· T R O P H I E S ·

Challenge
Copying Masters

Grade 4

Orlando   Boston   Dallas   Chicago   San Diego

Visit *The Learning Site!*
www.harcourtschool.com

ISBN 0-15-323525-X

7 8 9 10 076 10 09 08 07 06 05 04

Contents

LEAD THE WAY

The Gardener 1–3

Donavan's Word Jar 6–8

My Name Is María Isabel. 11–12

Lou Gehrig: The Luckiest Man 15–16

Amelia and Eleanor Go for a Ride 19–20

The Baker's Neighbor 24–26

The Emperor and the Kite. 29–30

Nights of the Pufflings 33–35

The Garden of Happiness 38–39

How to Babysit an Orangutan 42–43

Sarah, Plain and Tall. 46–48

Stealing Home 52–53

The Cricket in Times Square. 56–57

Two Lands, One Heart. 60–61

Look to the North: A Wolf Pup Diary. 64–65

The Kids' Invention Book 68–70

The Case of Pablo's Nose. 73–74

In the Days of King Adobe 77–79

Red Writing Hood. 82–83

One Grain of Rice 86–87

Fire! 90–92

A Very Important Day 95–97

Saguaro Cactus. 100–101

Blue Willow 104–106

In My Family 109–110

Gold Rush 113–115

I Have Heard of a Land 118–120

Paul Bunyan and Babe the Blue Ox 123–124

Fly Traps! Plants That Bite Back 127–128

The Down and Up Fall 131–132

Answer Key. A1

A Garden of Words

Start a word garden! Think of words that are connected to the Vocabulary Words in different ways.

| anxious | recognizing | adore | vacant | sprucing | retire |

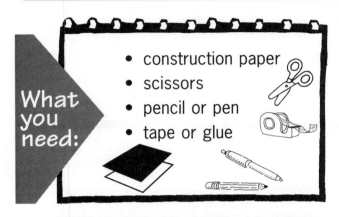

What you need:
- construction paper
- scissors
- pencil or pen
- tape or glue

Same   Opposite   Go Together

What to do:

1. Draw a flowerpot shape on three pieces of brown or red construction paper, and cut out each shape. On one flower pot, write *Same*. On the second, write *Opposite*, and on the third, write *Go Together*.

2. Cut 18 green construction paper strips. Tape or paste 6 strips to the top of each flowerpot as if they were the stems of flowers. Write one Vocabulary Word on each strip. Each pot should hold 6 plant stems, each labeled with one of the six Vocabulary Words.

3. Cut 18 flower shapes out of different-colored construction paper. Tape, paste, or staple the flowers to the top of the stems in each pot.

4. On each of the flowers in the flowerpot labeled *Same*, write a synonym—a word with the same meaning. On each of the flowers in the pot labeled *Opposite*, write an antonym—a word with the opposite meaning. On each of the flowers in the pot labeled *Go Together*, write another word that you think of when you hear the Vocabulary Word.

© Harcourt

Challenge
Lead the Way

Frame a Story

Setting, characters, and plot are the basic elements of every story. Think about the setting, characters, and plot of "The Gardener." Then use these narrative elements to retell the ending in story frames.

What you need:

- white paper
- pencil or pen

- markers or colored pencils

What to do:

1. Take notes about the setting, characters, and important events on pages 40–43 of "The Gardener."

2. Fold a strip of paper into four squares, or frames. Decide which characters and events will be in each frame.

3. Draw a picture in each frame for the events on pages 40–43 of the story. Make sure the background of each picture frame reflects the setting. Carefully draw each character.

4. Use speech balloons for the words of the characters' dialogue.

Challenge
Lead the Way

© Harcourt

Fill in the Gaps

What can you do when an author doesn't tell you everything you want
to know? You can use story clues and what you already know to make
an inference!

What you need:

- white paper
- pencil or pen
- markers or colored pencils

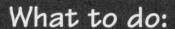

What to do:

1. Reread "The Gardener," and find a place where you go beyond the text and make an inference.

2. Fold a sheet of drawing paper into three sections. At the top of the left section, write *Story Clues*. Then list the clues the author gives you. Illustrate one clue.

3. Label the center section *What I Know*. In this section, write something you already know about the topic from your own experience. Add an illustration.

4. Title the right section *My Inference*. In this section, write your inference, using the story clues and what you already know. Add an illustration.

Challenge
Lead the Way

Memory Clues

One way to remember something for a long time is to link the information with a picture. You can use this strategy to create memory clues for your Vocabulary Words.

| leisure | disappointment | perseverance |
| uneasy | compromise | chortle |

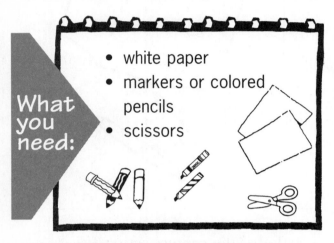

What you need:

- white paper
- markers or colored pencils
- scissors

Compromise
to reach an agreement after each side gives up part of its demands

What to do:

1. Review the Vocabulary Words and definitions from "Donavan's Word Jar." Think about what each word means. In your mind, picture a person, a place, an activity, or another scene that reminds you of the Vocabulary Word.

2. Fold and cut each sheet of paper into four equal sections. Cut the sections apart.

3. On each section, write one Vocabulary Word and its definition. On the other side of the paper, draw your memory clue.

4. Use your pictures to study your words. Look at each picture. Name the word, and give its definition. Turn the picture over to check whether you were correct.

Challenge
Lead the Way

Word Race

A prefix is a word part that is added to the beginning of a word to change the word's meaning. A suffix is a word part that changes the meaning of a word when added to the end of the word. Construct new words using prefixes, suffixes, and root words.

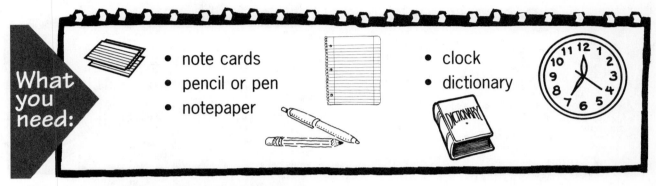

What you need:

- note cards
- pencil or pen
- notepaper
- clock
- dictionary

What to do:

1. Write each prefix, suffix, and root word on one side of a note card and its definition on the other side.

2. Use the word parts to construct as many new words as you can in five minutes. Write the words on a sheet of paper.

3. After five minutes, stop writing. Count how many words you have made. Use a dictionary to confirm meaning.

4. Write each of your new words in a sentence.

Prefixes		Suffixes		Root Words
un-	not	*-ful*	full of	refine
re-	again	*-able*	capable of	self
mis-	wrongly	*-er*	one who	present
pre-	before	*-less*	without	sense
over-	over	*-ment*	action of	fortune
dis-	not	*-ish*	with the qualities of	content

© Harcourt

7

Name _____

Word Wheels

Using synonyms and antonyms can keep your writing lively and make it more precise. A synonym is a word that has the same or almost the same meaning as another word. An antonym is a word with the opposite or nearly the opposite meaning of another word.

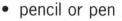

What you need:

- three paper plates or sheets of heavy paper
- paper fastener

- pencil or pen
- thesaurus or dictionary

What to do:

1. Select four words from "Donavan's Word Jar" or from your own writing.

2. Find at least one synonym and one antonym for each word on your list. Use a thesaurus or dictionary to help you.

3. Cut three circles from the paper plates or paper. Make each a different size. Attach the circles together at the center with a paper fastener. Draw lines to divide the circles into equal sections. Write a word from your list in each section of the smallest circle.

4. Write antonyms for each word in a section of the second circle. Write synonyms for each word in a section of the outer circle. Turn the word wheel to line up a word with its synonyms and antonyms.

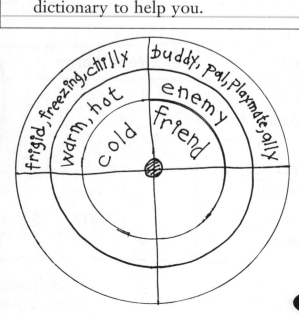

8

© Harcourt

Building Word Pyramids

One way to understand a word is to recognize its parts. Many words contain a base word plus a prefix, a suffix, or both. Another way to learn about a word is to think about the words that are related to it.

| pageant | rehearsals | restless |
| troublesome | tropical | attentively |

What you need:

- notepaper
- pencil or pen

- markers or colored pencils
- dictionary

What to do:

1. Write the Vocabulary Words on a sheet of paper. Next to each word, write its definition. Use a dictionary if you need to.

2. Look carefully at the vocabulary words. Underline each root word. You can use a dictionary if you aren't sure what the root words are.

3. Copy each root word on a separate sheet of paper. Below the root word, write words that contain the root word plus a prefix. Below that, write words that contain the root word plus a suffix. At the bottom of the pyramid, write words that contain the root word plus both a prefix and a suffix.

4. Write a definition for one of the new words you listed in your pyramid at the bottom of each page. Draw a large triangle around the words on each page. Decorate each page with drawings that illustrate the words.

Challenge
Lead the Way

Design a Book Cover

One place people learn about the characters, setting, and plot of a book is from its cover. Think about the covers of your favorite books. Then follow the steps below to make a cover for "My Name Is María Isabel."

What you need:
- sheet of white paper
- pencil or pen
- markers or colored pencils

What to do:

1. Take notes on the main character, setting, and plot. Who is the main character? What is she like? Where does most of the action take place? What happens? What problems does the main character face? How does she solve them?

2. Fold the piece of paper in half. Lay it before you with the crease on the left.

3. On the front cover, draw a picture that shows the setting, the main character, and one of the main character's problems. Write the title of the book and the name of the author.

4. On the back cover, tell about the main character. Describe her situation and the problems she faces. Then write a question or a sentence that will make others want to read the book.

Scavenger Hunt

A scavenger hunt is a game in which the players hunt for items from a list. In this version, you need to find the correct Vocabulary Word to fit each description in the list below. Use a dictionary to help you find the answers.

immigrants	**salary**	**modest**	**valuable**
appreciation	**courageous**	**tremendous**	**sportsmanship**

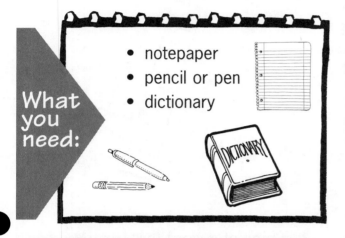

What you need:
- notepaper
- pencil or pen
- dictionary

What to do:

1. Find a word that can be both a noun and an adjective.
Find a word that is made up of three smaller words.

2. If you rearrange the letters of this word, you can spell two new words. One new word means a frightening creature, and one means a hill of sand.

3. Find a word that comes from a Latin root meaning *price*.

Find a word that has something to do with the meaning of the word *mettle*.

4. If you rearrange the letters of this word, you can spell three new words. One new word is a pronoun, one is a type of candy, and one is a unit of measure.

5. Find a word whose Latin origin has something to do with the word *salt*.
If you take off the first letter and the last two letters of this word, the word you have left is a type of poem.

Challenge
Lead the Way

Word Chains

Many words share the same prefixes or suffixes. Some words have both prefixes and suffixes that they share with other words. You can show some of these shared prefixes and suffixes by creating word chains.

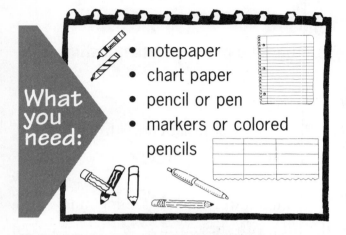

What you need:

- notepaper
- chart paper
- pencil or pen
- markers or colored pencils

What to do:

1. Make a list of prefixes and a list of suffixes. Then list words with prefixes, words with suffixes, and words with both.

2. On a sheet of chart paper, write a word with a prefix. Write the word from left to right, with each letter of the word in a separate square.

3. Think of a word that has the same prefix as the first word and has a suffix. Write the word from top to bottom, connecting it to the first word by a letter in the shared prefix.

4. Think of a word that has the same suffix as the second word. Write the word from left to right, connecting it to the second word by a letter in the shared suffix. Make as many word chains as you can. Use additional sheets of chart paper if necessary.

© Harcourt

Challenge
Lead the Way

Dial a Definition

Use the Vocabulary Words from "Amelia and Eleanor Go for a Ride" to create a definition dial.

outspoken	practical	elegant	elevations
starstruck	miniatures	brisk	marveled

What you need:

- notepaper
- construction paper
- pencil or pen
- drawing compass or three round objects
- scissors
- paper fastener or paper clip
- ruler or straightedge
- dictionary or thesaurus

What to do:

1. Write the Vocabulary Words on a sheet of paper. Write a definition for each one. Use a dictionary or thesaurus to find an antonym for each word.

2. With a drawing compass, draw three circles of different sizes on three sheets of construction paper. Cut out the circles. Then use your drawing compass or a pencil to punch small holes carefully in the centers of each of the circles. Stack the three circles, with the largest on the bottom and the smallest on top.

3. Join the three circles with a paper clip. Draw a line from the center of the smallest circle to the outer edge of the biggest circle. Draw seven more lines like the first line, making eight equal sections.

4. Write one of the Vocabulary Words in each section of the smallest circle. Write antonyms for each of the Vocabulary Words in the sections of the middle circle. Write a definition for each word in each section of the largest circle. Rotate the circles to line up a Vocabulary Word with its definition and antonym.

Challenge
Lead the Way

Name _____

A Biography of a Star

The stars in the sky are not the only kind of stars. There are stars on Earth as well. You can learn more about a famous person by locating information and using it to write a biography.

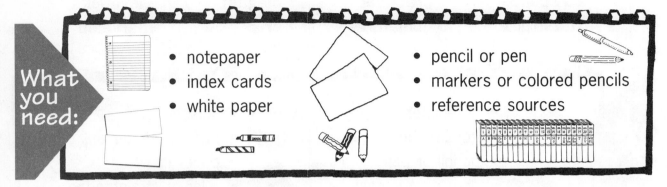

What you need:

- notepaper
- index cards
- white paper

- pencil or pen
- markers or colored pencils
- reference sources

What to do:

1. Choose a famous person who you would like to research. Identify reference sources you can use, such as books, encyclopedias, magazines, and the Internet. List the reference sources in order, from the one you think will be the most useful to the one you think will be the least useful.

2. Start at the top of your list. Try to find information about your subject from the different reference sources. Use the tables of contents, glossaries, and indexes to help you find the information you want. Write the most important information on index cards.

3. Evaluate the type and amount of information you found in each reference source. Think about how easy each reference source was to use. Give each reference source a usefulness rating, with five stars for an excellent source and one star for a poor source.

4. Write a short biography of your subject. On a sheet of white paper, draw a picture of the person. Use your picture as the cover page of your biography.

Challenge
Lead the Way

Name _____

Word Mobile

Increase your understanding of each Vocabulary Word by thinking of words you associate with it. Then create a word mobile.

privilege	**luxury**	**shiftless**	**assent**
shamefacedly	**elated**	**indignantly**	**ad lib**

What you need:

- pencil or pen
- markers or colored pencils
- notepaper
- construction paper

- string
- coat hanger
- dictionary
- thesaurus

What to do:

1. Cut out 16 circles from construction paper of different colors, two from each color. Make sure that the circles are large enough to write a word on.

2. Write each Vocabulary Word on a circle of a different color.

3. Brainstorm words you associate with each Vocabulary Word. Choose one for each and write it on a circle of the same color.

4. Make holes in each circle with a hole punch or scissors. Attach each vocabulary word to its related word with string. Tie the words to a coat hanger.

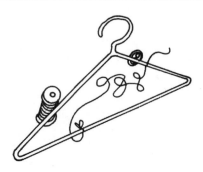

© Harcourt

Challenge
Lead the Way

A Batch of Causes and Effects

What happens in "The Baker's Neighbor," and why does it happen? Mix up a batch of causes and effects from the selection. To find an effect, ask *What happened?* To find a cause, ask *Why did this happen?*

What you need:

- construction paper
- scissors
- tape or glue

- poster board
- pencil or pen

What to do:

1. Reread "The Baker's Neighbor," and choose at least four different cause-and-effect relationships in the story. Remember that a cause can have more than one effect and an effect can have more than one cause.

2. Cut out mixing bowl shapes, and write each cause on a separate shape. Cut out pie slice shapes, and write each effect on a separate shape.

3. Arrange the shapes on a piece of poster board to show the different cause-and-effect relationships. Paste down the shapes. Draw an arrow from each cause to each of its effects.

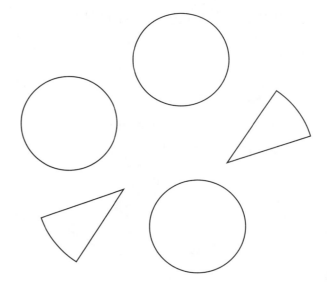

© Harcourt

Challenge
Lead the Way

Name _____

Paint a Portrait

Figurative language can be used to describe a person. A simile is a comparison that uses *like* or *as*. A metaphor is a comparison that says that one thing *is* another. Use similes and metaphors to paint portraits of the main characters in "The Baker's Neighbor."

What you need:

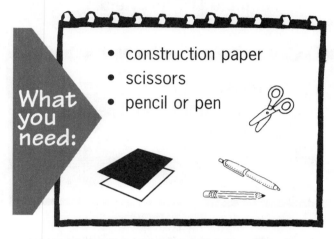

- construction paper
- scissors
- pencil or pen

What to do:

1. Reread "The Baker's Neighbor," and look for references to Manuel and Pablo.

2. When you are familiar with the characters, write sentences that use similes or metaphors to describe each character.

3. Cut two pieces of construction paper of different colors into two face shapes.

4. Label one face *Manuel* and the other *Pablo*. Then copy the sentences you wrote about each character onto each face.

Challenge
Lead the Way

Name _____

A Word Kite

Djeow Seow used a kite to rescue her father. You can make a kite and use it to help you learn about the Vocabulary Words.

| insignificant | loyal | plotting | twined |
| steely | encircling | neglected | yielding |

What you need:

- poster board
- construction paper
- pencil or pen
- ruler or straightedge

- scissors
- markers or colored pencils
- tape or glue
- dictionary

What to do:

1. Cut the poster board into a large diamond shape, like a kite. Using the ruler or straightedge, draw a line connecting the top corner and the bottom corner. Then draw a line connecting the two side corners. Do the same thing on the back of the poster board.

2. Now your kite has four sections on each side. With a marker or colored pencil, write a Vocabulary Word in each section. Under each Vocabulary Word, write its definition in a different color. You can use a dictionary to help you.

3. Under each definition, use a third color to make a list of words that have the same meaning as the Vocabulary Word. In a fourth color, add words to the lists that mean the opposite of each Vocabulary Word.

4. In each section, draw a picture that helps you remember the meaning of the Vocabulary Word.

5. Use strips of construction paper to make a tail for your kite. On the tail, write two sentences using Vocabulary Words. Tape or glue the tail to your kite.

Challenge
Lead the Way

Name _____

Narrative Elements Pinwheel

Have you ever thought about how narrative elements work together in a story? Sometimes changes in setting or character can affect the plot. Follow the instructions below to explore the relationships between narrative elements.

What you need:
- notepaper
- construction paper
- pencil or pen
- scissors
- paper fastener or paper clip
- ruler or straightedge

What to do:

1. Cut three squares of different sizes from construction paper. Punch a small hole in the center of each square.

2. Place the squares on top of each other, with the largest square on bottom and the smallest on top. Join the three squares with a paper fastener or a paper clip.

3. Draw a line from the center of the smallest square to the outer edge of the largest square. Draw two more lines like the first line, making three equal sections.

4. Think of three stories. Use information from the stories to fill in the sections on your squares.
- In each section of the smallest square, list the main character of each of the three stories.
- In each section of the middle square, tell when and where each story takes place.
- In each section of the largest square, describe the main events.

5. Rotate the middle square until the settings line up with different stories. Would the plots of the stories be different if the settings were different? Then rotate the character square. How would the plot change if the characters were different?

© Harcourt

30

"Finding" a Poem

One way to write a poem is to use words that you find in something you have read. Use words from "Nights of the Pufflings" to write a poem about a topic that interests you.

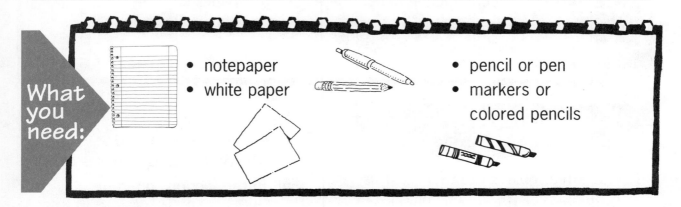

uninhabited	burrows	venture
stranded	nestles	instinctively

What you need:

- notepaper
- white paper

- pencil or pen
- markers or colored pencils

What to do:

1. Look through "Nights of the Pufflings," and make a list of interesting words. Include the Vocabulary Words.

2. Play around with the words, arranging them in a meaningful way. Think of what you want to say, and add any extra words that your poem needs to make sense.

3. Copy your poem on another sheet of paper. Illustrate your poem and share it.

Challenge
Lead the Way

Aboard the Summary Train

A good summary is like a train—it starts at the beginning and follows through to the end. Create a summary train to help you write a summary of a nonfiction article that you choose.

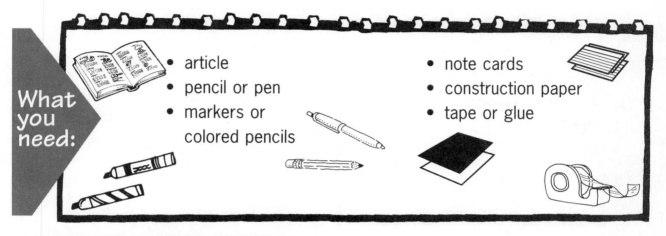

What you need:

- article
- pencil or pen
- markers or colored pencils
- note cards
- construction paper
- tape or glue

What to do:

1. Read the selection. Decide what the main idea of the whole selection is. Write the main idea, including the author's purpose, on a note card.

2. Decide how to separate the selection into sections. Then determine how each section is organized. Write the main idea of each section on separate note cards. Under the main idea, write only the details in that section that directly relate to the main idea of that section.

3. On another card, write as your summary's ending your opinion about the article.

4. Cut out a train engine, train cars, and a caboose from different colors of construction paper. You should cut out as many train cars as you have sections in your book or article. Tape or glue the note cards onto the train parts. Use markers or colored pencils to decorate your train.

5. Now write a paragraph to summarize the selection. Use all the ideas and details from your summary train.

Searching for Glaciers

Part of Iceland is covered by glaciers. What are glaciers? Where do they come from? How do they develop? Do they ever melt? Use different resources to research glaciers.

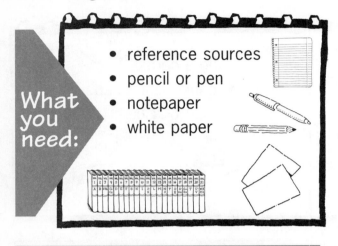

What you need:

- reference sources
- pencil or pen
- notepaper
- white paper

What to do:

1. Write a list of your research questions about glaciers. You may use those suggested above or create your own.

2. Identify the resources available in your classroom. These might include an encyclopedia, the Internet, and an atlas. Copy this chart on white paper. Be sure to leave enough room to fill in the chart.

	Encyclopedia	Internet	Atlas
What key words to use			
Kinds of information I found			

3. Fill in each part of the chart. Answer these questions:
   - What key words do I use to find this information?
   - What specific kinds of information can I find in each source?

4. After you have completed the chart, evaluate the research process. Answer these questions:
   - Which source gave me the most information?
   - Which source was easiest to use?
   - What problems did I have searching for information?
   - What can I do to solve those problems?

5. What advice would you give to someone else who was doing research? Use your evaluation to write a *be sure to* checklist for search techniques.

© Harcourt

Challenge
Lead the Way

Name _____

A Garden of Words

Marisol and her neighbors grew vegetables and flowers in their garden. Try your hand at growing a word garden.

| inhaled | lavender | mural | skidded | haze |

What you need:

- white paper
- construction paper

- markers or colored pencils
- tape or glue

What to do:

1. On a sheet of white paper, draw a border for a garden. Cut strips of brown construction paper for the soil. Cut strips of green construction paper for grass and plants. Tape or glue the brown and green strips to your garden plot.

2. Cut eight flowers from construction paper. On each flower, write a different Vocabulary Word.

3. Tape or glue the flowers to your garden. Leave the bottom of the flower loose so that you can lift it to write underneath. Write the definition for each word under the flower to which it belongs.

4. Use your garden to help you study your words.

lavender · inhaled · mural · skidded · haze

Challenge
Lead the Way

How Does Your Garden Grow?

Identifying cause-and-effect relationships can help you better understand how and why things happen. In "The Garden of Happiness," Marisol plants a sunflower seed. Because of her action, a sunflower plant grows. Make a memory game to connect causes in "The Garden of Happiness" with their effects.

What you need:

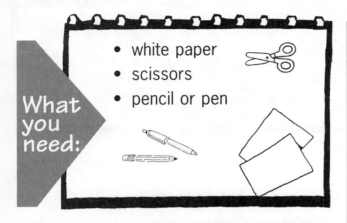

- white paper
- scissors
- pencil or pen

What to do:

1. Fold a sheet of white paper in half. Fold it in half again. Fold it in half a third time. Open the paper. The paper should be divided into eight sections. Repeat the process with a second sheet of paper.

2. Look in "The Garden of Happiness" for eight cause-and-effect relationships. Write each cause in a section on the left side of your folded paper. On the right side of the paper, write the effects. Cut the paper along the fold lines to separate each cause and effect.

3. Place the *cause* cards and the *effect* cards face down on your desk. Mix them up.

4. Turn over two cards. If the cards match the cause with its effect, keep them. If they don't match, turn the cards face down again. Keep playing until you match each cause with its effect.

Marisol plants a sunflower seed.

A sunflower plant grows.

Challenge
Lead the Way

© Harcourt

Name _____

Creative Acrostic

You've probably written acrostic poems before, but this one will be all about you. It also will help you learn your new Vocabulary Words. Make sure to read all of the steps before you begin writing your poem, or you may miss some important instructions.

endangered   smuggled   jealous   displeasure   facial   coordination

What you need:

- one sheet of construction paper
- markers or colored pencils
- notepaper
- pencil or pen

What to do:

1. Choose your first, last, or full name to use as the main word in the acrostic. Write the name vertically on your notepaper, and leave a blank line between each letter.

2. Beside each letter, write a sentence that describes something about you. The letter of your name that is on that line will be the first letter of the first word of that sentence. For example, if you are using SARAH, *S* will be the first letter of the first word of the first sentence. The letter *A* will be the first letter of the first word of the second sentence, and so on.

3. As you write your sentences, use each of the Vocabulary Words. You don't have to use a Vocabulary Word in every sentence, but make sure you use each word at least once.

4. When you are satisfied with your acrostic, copy it onto the construction paper, using markers or colored pencils. You may want to experiment by making the letters of your name stand out. Underline the Vocabulary Words with a special color.

Challenge
Lead the Way

Name _____

A Week in the Life

You will be creating a "Week in the Life" book about yourself.

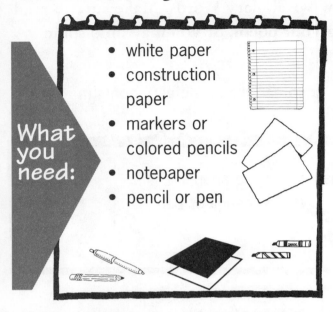

What you need:

- white paper
- construction paper
- markers or colored pencils
- notepaper
- pencil or pen

What to do:

1. Think about a week in your life that was full of different activities. List on your notepaper six or seven important events that took place that week. For example, "I went to Matt's birthday party; my cat had kittens; my cousin Jack came over; we won our baseball game." Try to remember the day of the week each event happened, and list the days.

2. Summarize the most important information you remember about each event. For example, you could write the following: "I went to Matt's birthday party. We had all my favorite foods. I won the softball throw contest and a ticket to rent a free video!"

3. Fold the construction paper to make a book. Fold the unlined paper, and place it inside. Decorate the front of your book with the title "A Week in the Life of (your name)" and drawings of things you like.

4. Place each of the events in the order they happened, and copy them neatly onto the unlined paper in your book. If you use the front and back of the folded paper, you will have four sheets to write on.

© Harcourt

Challenge
Lead the Way

Name _____

Analogy Sort

Analogies show the relationships between two pairs of words. The words in each pair are related in the same way. For example, both pairs of words may be opposites. They may both be parts of a whole. They may show cause and effect.

| alarmed | windbreak | conch | paddock | rustle |

What you need:

- notepaper
- pencil or pen
- dictionary and thesaurus

What to do:

1. Copy the chart below onto a sheet of notepaper.

Vocabulary Word	Same	Opposite
alarmed	scared	calm

2. Write each Vocabulary Word in the first column.

3. Use a thesaurus to find a word that represents the relationship shown in each column.

4. Use the information in the chart to write an analogy for each Vocabulary Word.

Challenge
Lead the Way

Conclusion Cards

Authors do not always tell all information in a story directly. Readers must use details in the story and their own knowledge to draw conclusions. In "Sarah, Plain and Tall," the author does not say directly that Sarah is homesick. Revisit the story and find text that supports this conclusion. Then make Conclusion Cards for the conclusions you drew about characters in "Sarah, Plain and Tall."

What you need:

- note cards
- pencil or pen

What to do:

Sarah is homesick.

Sarah looked out over the plains. There is no sea here, but the land rolls a little like the sea. Sarah is not smiling. From my own knowledge I know that homesick people miss the places where they grew up.

1. Reread "Sarah, Plain and Tall" to find places where details from the story and your own knowledge helped you draw conclusions.

2. Write each conclusion on a separate card. On the other side, write the details from the text and your own knowledge to support each conclusion.

3. Were you able to support all your conclusions? If not, modify the conclusion. Do all of your reasons support your conclusions? If not, remove the reason from your list.

4. Write a paragraph about your conclusions and the details and knowledge you needed to draw them.

Challenge
Lead the Way

Picturing the Prairie

Both nonfiction and fiction stories sometimes include maps, charts, diagrams, illustrations, or photographs. These graphic aids provide additional information to help readers understand the story. Make a diagram that shows what the prairie looks like and which plants and animals can be found there.

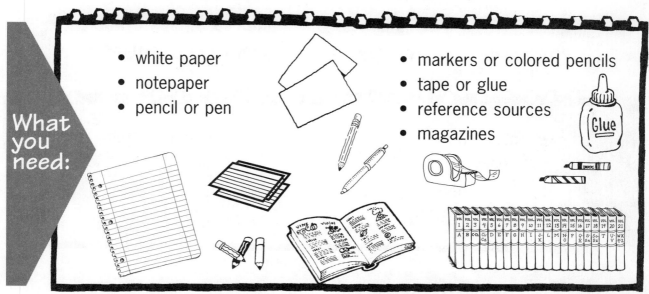

What you need:

- white paper
- notepaper
- pencil or pen

- markers or colored pencils
- tape or glue
- reference sources
- magazines

What to do:

1. Research the prairie. Look in encyclopedias, in books, and on the Internet to find out what the prairie looks like and what plants and animals can be found there.

2. On a large sheet of paper, draw a prairie setting. Add pictures of plants and animals from the prairie. You can draw pictures or cut them out of old magazines.

3. Write a caption describing each plant and animal on a separate slip of paper. Tape or glue each caption on your prairie diagram next to the plant or animal it describes.

4. Write a story to go along with your diagram.

Challenge
Lead the Way

The Terrific Ticket Giveaway

For which event would you like to have two free tickets? A concert? A college or professional sports event? A play or movie? Here's your chance to use your Vocabulary Words and your writing skills to win those tickets in the Terrific Ticket Giveaway.

glumly disposition	pastimes grudge	impose bicker	irritably tutor

What you need:

- dictionary
- notepaper
- pencil or pen

- markers or colored pencils

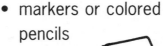

What to do:

1. Pick an event for which you would like to have two free tickets.

2. Write a short paragraph in which you tell the sponsors of the event why they should award you two free tickets.

3. Your entry will not be considered if any of the Vocabulary Words are used incorrectly. Use a dictionary to ensure that you have used each word correctly. Proofread your paragraph to catch any errors.

4. Underline each Vocabulary Word with a marker or colored pencil so the contest judges can see them easily.

Challenge
Lead the Way

Name _____

Far from Home

Imagine that you have the chance to visit a faraway place. Before you decide where to take your trip, you should research several places.

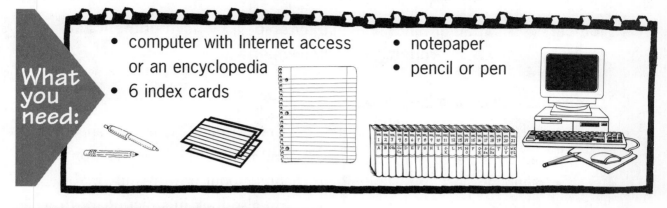

What you need:
- computer with Internet access or an encyclopedia
- 6 index cards
- notepaper
- pencil or pen

What to do:

1. Think of two faraway places you would like to visit.

2. Write the name of each place on an index card.

3. Use the Internet or encyclopedias to do your research. On the back of each card, record the following information about each place: 1) the location (country, continent, etc.); 2) the climate throughout the year; 3) places or events of interest.

4. Write a paragraph in which you compare or contrast the two places. Write a second paragraph telling which place you would rather visit and why.

Challenge
Lead the Way

Mapping Words

A lot of work goes into making a dictionary. Explore each of the Vocabulary Words in a word map. Then write your own dictionary entry.

logical	acquaintance	excitable	sympathetically
wistfully	eavesdropping	scrounging	

What you need:

- notepaper
- pencil or pen
- dictionary
- thesaurus

2. To figure out the part of speech, find the word in the selection, and think about how it is used. You can also look in a dictionary to find this information.

3. Write the Vocabulary Word's definition from the selection. Look in a dictionary to find other definitions for each word. Then use a thesaurus to find synonyms.

What to do:

1. Draw a word map like the one below for each Vocabulary Word. Write the Vocabulary Word in the center of the map.

4. List several related words in the map. Related words include other forms of the word and words with the same root.

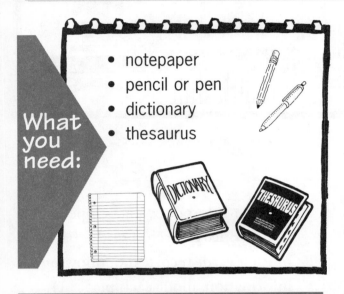

What part of speech is it?

What are some synonyms?

What are some related words?

What does it mean?

5. Choose one Vocabulary Word, and use your word map to create a dictionary entry for the word. In your dictionary entry, include a sentence that uses the Vocabulary Word.

Challenge
Lead the Way

Name _____

Don't Jump to Conclusions!

Authors don't always tell you everything you want to know about characters
and events in a story. That doesn't mean you have to jump to incorrect
conclusions, though. You can combine story information and your own
knowledge to draw a conclusion that makes sense.

What you need:

- construction paper
- poster board
- pencil or pen

- markers or colored pencils
- tape or glue

What to do:

1. Cut out two large circles from one color of construction paper and a large rectangle from another color. Label the circles *Story Information* and *What I Know*. Label the rectangle *My Conclusion*.

2. Find a passage in "The Cricket in Times Square" where you have to draw a conclusion because the author doesn't tell you everything you need or want to know.

3. Write the story information the author gives you on one circle. On the other circle, write what you already know. Use the story information and what you know to draw a conclusion. Write your conclusion on the rectangle.

4. Tape or glue the shapes on a piece of poster board. Draw a plus sign between the two circles and an arrow from the plus sign to the rectangle. Decorate your poster with a picture that illustrates the passage you chose.

© Harcourt

57

Word Family Trees

Most words are part of word families. Word families are groups of words
that have similar word parts. Often these words have related meanings, too.
Create a word family tree for each of the Vocabulary Words.

equivalent appetizing	interpreter overwhelm	irrigation hysterically	occasionally

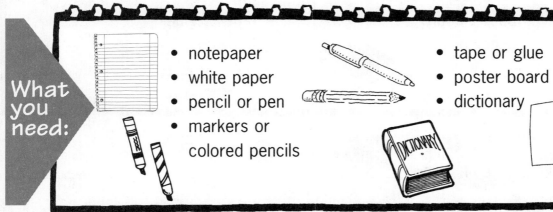

What you need:

- notepaper
- white paper
- pencil or pen
- markers or colored pencils

- tape or glue
- poster board
- dictionary

What to do:

1. Look up each Vocabulary Word in the dictionary. Find words that are related in spelling and meaning.

2. On white paper, draw seven trees with many branches. Write each Vocabulary Word on the trunk of a tree. Write related words on the branches.

3. Decorate the trees, and cut them out. Tape or glue the trees to a piece of poster board.

4. On slips of paper, write a sentence for each family tree, explaining how the words in that family are related. Tape or glue the slips under the trees on your poster.

© Harcourt

Challenge
Lead the Way

Name _____

Two States, One Country

In "Two Lands, One Heart," TJ compared and contrasted life in Vietnam with life in the United States. In the United States, there are similarities and differences between places, too. Find out how two states are alike and different through research.

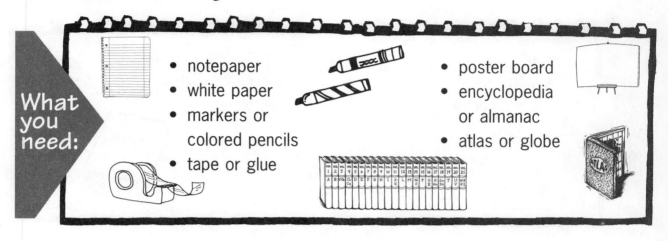

What you need:
- notepaper
- white paper
- markers or colored pencils
- tape or glue
- poster board
- encyclopedia or almanac
- atlas or globe

What to do:

1. Choose two different states to research. Read about your states in an encyclopedia, an almanac, or another reference source. Take notes as you read. Look for ways in which the states are alike. Look for ways in which they are different.

2. Draw or trace an outline map of each state. Then draw or trace an outline map of the United States.

3. On each state map, write facts about the state. Add details that show how the states are different.

4. On the map of the United States, write facts that show how the states are alike.

5. Glue your maps to a sheet of poster board. Write a title for your poster. Share what you learned with the class.

© Harcourt

61

Create a Flyer

Imagine that you are looking for a lost pet. Use the Vocabulary Words to create a flyer that describes the pet.

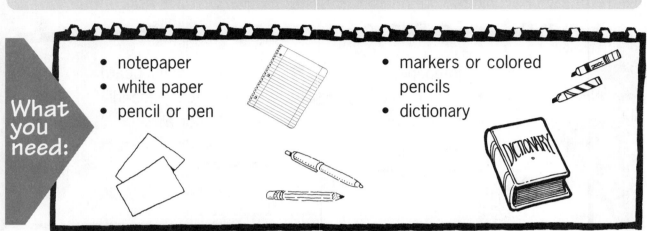

| tundra | ceases | bonding | piteously | surrender | abundant |

What you need:

- notepaper
- white paper
- pencil or pen

- markers or colored pencils
- dictionary

What to do:

1. Study the list of Vocabulary Words. Write each word and its definition on a sheet of notepaper. Try to write the definitions from memory. If you can't, use a dictionary to find the meanings. Then write the heading *Lost* on the white sheet of paper.

2. Use the Vocabulary Words to describe the pet. What does it look like? To what name does it answer? Does it know any special tricks? What is its favorite food? Where was the pet seen last?

3. Use markers or colored pencils to draw a picture of the pet. Offer a reward for its return. Include a phone number or address where you can be reached.

© Harcourt

Challenge
Lead the Way

A Comic-Strip Summary

When you summarize part of a story, you tell about the most important points. In this exercise, you will summarize parts of "Look to the North" and use your summaries to create a comic strip.

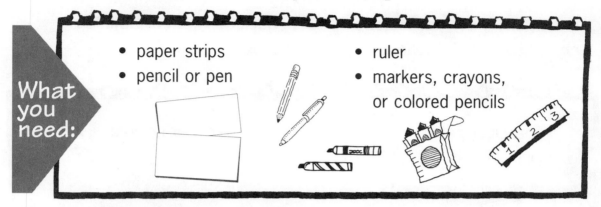

What you need:

- paper strips
- pencil or pen
- ruler
- markers, crayons, or colored pencils

What to do:

1. Choose four entries from "Look to the North: A Wolf Pup Diary." Write a brief summary of each entry.

3. Present your comic strip to the class. Read the captions, and explain how you chose topics for your drawings.

2. Fold a strip of paper into four squares. Label the squares with the headings from the days you summarized. On each square, draw a picture of the most important event that happened on that day. Use the ruler to draw lines beneath each picture. Write your summary of that day on the lines.

Challenge
Lead the Way

Word History Book

Every word has a history. Some words may have a long history, with origins in Greek and Roman times. Others may have a short history, such as computer-related words. What history do your Vocabulary Words have?

| document | prosthetic | device | disabilities |
| circular | scholarship | modify | |

What you need:

- pencil or pen
- index cards
- notepaper

- markers or colored pencils
- dictionary

What to do:

1. Write each Vocabulary Word on an index card. Look up each word in the dictionary.

2. Use the other side of the index card to take notes on the Vocabulary Word. Look for information about word origins, usage, variations in spelling, and any unusual phrases that contain the word. Remember that some words have root words. You may have to look up information on the root word to find all the information you need about the Vocabulary Word.

3. Write the word on a sheet of notepaper. Use markers or colored pencils to illustrate the word, or use fancy lettering to make the word stand out. Then write a paragraph about the word's history.

4. Keep your word histories in your notebook. You may wish to add other word histories as you learn new words.

Challenge
Lead the Way

Name _____

Invention Convention

Suppose your school has decided to have an Invention Convention in which students bring in and display their inventions. You are in charge of making a flyer for students. In the flyer, you need to give guidelines for creating inventions, as well as information about the convention.

What you need:

- pencil or pen
- white paper
- construction paper

- markers or colored pencils

What to do:

1. Look back over "The Kids' Invention Book," especially the section about creating your own invention. Take notes on the invention process. Write down examples of inventions that kids have already made.

2. Identify the main ideas of the invention process. Answer these questions: What do kids need to know to get started? What do they need to know to complete their projects? Use the examples of inventions to support your main ideas.

3. Create a *who, what, where,* and *when* introduction. Include all the details students need to know about the convention.

4. Print your information on the white paper. Announce the information about the convention at the top. Then number your main ideas about the invention process. Remember to put the ideas in a logical order. Add examples of student inventions where they are needed. Use markers or colored pencils to illustrate your flyer.

© Harcourt

Challenge
Lead the Way

Name _____

Daily Directions

Every day we complete many tasks, such as making a bed, packing a lunch, or saving files on a computer. Think of a task that you do every day. How would you explain that task to someone who may be unfamiliar with it?

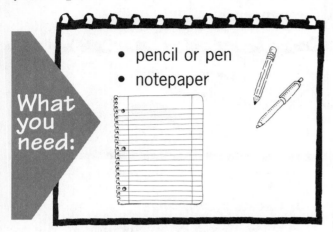

What you need:
- pencil or pen
- notepaper

What to do:

1. Brainstorm some tasks that you do every day. Choose one to explain.

2. Write down the steps that are needed to complete the task. Remember that you are explaining this task to someone who is unfamiliar with it. The person will follow your directions to complete the task. Arrange the steps in the correct sequence, using sequence words to guide the reader from one step to the next.

3. Tell whether completing the task requires any special information or skills. Then suggest ways people might find this information or learn these skills so that they can perform the task.

4. If people were to need help completing the task, whom should they ask? Write down a list of people who could help. Then write down any other sources that might help them with this task.

5. Write a checklist of important things to remember when completing the task.

© Harcourt

Challenge
Lead the Way

Get Nosy About Words

Words don't just appear out of nowhere. Every word has a history. Think of your own theories about what some words originally meant or where they came from. Then check your theories by doing some detective work using a dictionary.

| muttered | strengthening | sculptor |
| straightaway | retorted | alibi |

What you need:

- notepaper
- note cards
- pencil or pen
- dictionary

What to do:

1. Review the Vocabulary Words and their meanings. Write each word on a note card.

2. Brainstorm a list of theories about each word's origin. Be creative! Use any knowledge you have of foreign languages. Write your theories about the words' origins on the note cards.

3. Look up each word in the dictionary. Write information from the dictionary about each word's actual origin on the cards. Compare your ideas with the word origins shown in the dictionary. How close were you to the actual word origins?

Challenge
Lead the Way

A Nose for Sequence

Events in most stories are told in the order in which they happen. Paying attention to the sequence of events, or time order, will help you understand the story. In "The Case of Pablo's Nose," the sequence of events begins with the theft of Pablo's nose sculpture. It ends when the thief is caught. Make a sequence of noses to show the order of events in "The Case of Pablo's Nose."

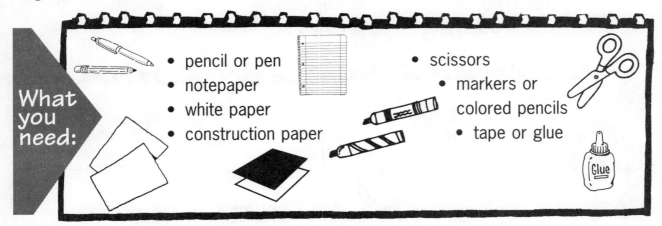

What you need:

- pencil or pen
- notepaper
- white paper
- construction paper
- scissors
- markers or colored pencils
- tape or glue

What to do:

1. Draw the outlines of several noses on a piece of white paper. Each one should be large enough that you can write something and draw a picture on it. Cut out the nose outlines.

2. Make a list of the events in the story, starting with the theft of the nose. Copy each event onto a separate nose. Do not number them. Decorate each nose with an illustration of the event.

3. Turn over the noses. Mix them up. Flip them back over, with the events showing. Lay them out on your desk in the order in which the events occurred.

4. Tape or glue the noses onto a piece of construction paper. Display your creations in the classroom.

© Harcourt

Challenge
Lead the Way

Name _____

Super Spy Decoder

You can create a secret code to exchange messages with your friends. Don't let
your Super Spy Decoder fall into the wrong hands!

| fascinated | thrifty | generous | roguish | rascally |

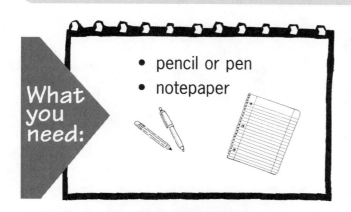

- pencil or pen
- notepaper

What you need:

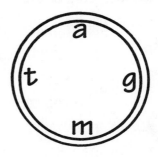

What to do:

1. Write one original sentence for each Vocabulary Word. Make sure each sentence shows the meaning of the word.

2. List all the letters of the alphabet on another piece of paper. Directly across from each letter, write a different letter or symbol. Do not use any letters or symbols twice, or your decoder will not work.

3. Use your new code to rewrite all of your sentences. Leave a blank where each Vocabulary Word goes.

4. Share your decoder and coded sentences with a friend. See if he or she can decode your sentences and fill in each blank with the correct Vocabulary Word.

Challenge
Lead the Way

Name _____

I Want to Be Your Next Mayor!

Suppose that you decided to run for mayor of your city or town. How would you earn votes? You'd convince people that you were the best candidate by focusing on an important issue. Think of the issue as your main idea, and think of your specific plan as the details.

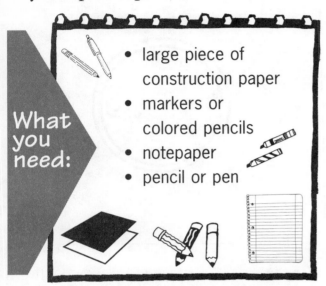

What you need:

- large piece of construction paper
- markers or colored pencils
- notepaper
- pencil or pen

What to do:

1. Brainstorm the most important ideas you want to address in your campaign.

2. Choose the main idea that interests you most or that will convince the most people to vote for you.

3. Design a campaign poster that explains this idea. List details that show you have thought about the issue and have a plan that you can carry out.

4. Write your name and the name of the office for which you are running. Decorate your poster so that it will be eye-catching.

Challenge
Lead the Way

Name _____

I Wonder Why

Science explains many mysteries for us now, but long ago, people had to create their own answers. They told stories to explain things. Their stories, called myths, also expressed ideas, values, and emotions. Write a myth to explain something you wonder about. Use the following myth told by the Yoruba people of Nigeria as a model.

Olokun, the god of the sea, lived in a splendid underwater palace and was attended by humans and fish. Long ago, Olokun challenged the sky god, Olorun, to a contest to decide who was the supreme ruler. They agreed to a contest in which the god with the most magnificent robes would be declared the winner.

On the contest day, Olokun arrived to compete, but Olorun sent Chameleon to compete on his behalf. No matter how splendid a garment Olokun put on, Chameleon matched it exactly. Finally, Olokun gave up and declared Olorun the winner.

To this day, the sky has power over the seas and their tides.

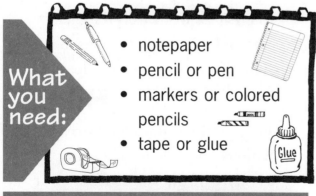

What you need:
- notepaper
- pencil or pen
- markers or colored pencils
- tape or glue

What to do:

1. Brainstorm a list of things that you have wondered about. These can be things for which you know the explanations or things for which you don't.

2. Choose one thing you've wondered about to use as the subject of your myth. Decide who the characters in your myth will be.

3. Write a myth that explains the thing you've wondered about and that also expresses your ideas, values, or emotions. Create an illustration to accompany your myth.

Challenge
Lead the Way

Name _____

Word Webs

To remember a word, it sometimes helps to think of related words. Create word webs for the Vocabulary Words, and use them to write a skit.

What you need:

- pencil
- markers or colored pencils
- paper

What to do:

1. For each Vocabulary Word, brainstorm and list words that are related to it.

2. Reread your list of words, and underline verbs in one color, adjectives in another color, and nouns in a third color.

3. Use your list of related words to create a word web for each Vocabulary Word. Give each type of word its own circle.

4. Write a short skit based on a famous tale of your choosing. Use as many of the words from your word webs as you can. Ask a classmate to help you perform your skit.

© Harcourt

Challenge
Lead the Way

A Sequence Chain

Most stories are organized chronologically, or in time order. Words such as *first, then, next,* and *finally* are often used to signal the sequence of events, or the order in which they happen. Use these and other signal words to make a sequence chain to tell what happens in "Red Writing Hood" or another favorite story.

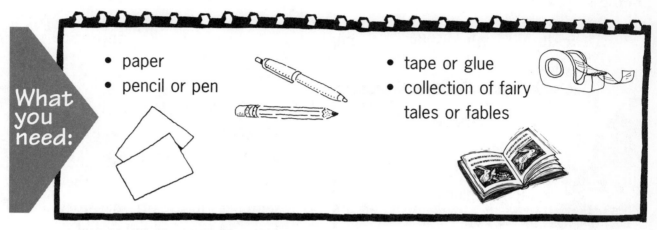

What you need:

- paper
- pencil or pen

- tape or glue
- collection of fairy tales or fables

What to do:

1. Reread "Red Writing Hood," or select another tale to read. List the events of the story in time order.

2. Cut a strip of paper for each event you have listed. Write one event on each strip. Arrange the strips in sequence, or the order in which the events happened.

3. Brainstorm a list of words and phrases that signal sequence. Turn each event strip over, and write a signal word or phrase that correctly describes the event's place in the order of events.

4. Beginning with the first event, and continuing in order, tape or glue the strips together as links in a chain. The outside of the links in the chain should show the sequence words and phrases.

© Harcourt

83

Challenge
Lead the Way

A Word from Our News Reporter

Adding new words to your vocabulary can help make your writing more interesting and more precise. News reporters use exact language to present their stories in the most accurate and interesting ways. Try your hand at being a reporter.

trickle	plentifully	implored	famine	decreed

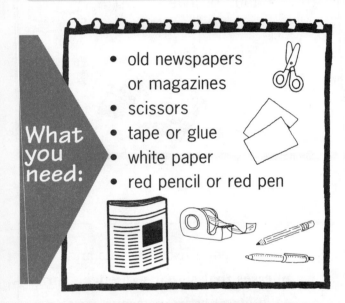

What you need:

- old newspapers or magazines
- scissors
- tape or glue
- white paper
- red pencil or red pen

What to do:

1. Scan the newspaper to find a short article that interests you. Cut out the article, and tape or glue it to a sheet of paper.

2. Find sentences in the news article in which you can substitute the Vocabulary Words.

3. Revise the article to include the Vocabulary Words. You can delete words, insert new text, or rearrange the order of the sentences in the original story. Use a red pen or red pencil to make proofreading marks in the margins of your paper to show your changes.

4. Write five more sentences for the article. Use five Vocabulary Words from an earlier reading selection.

5. When you have revised your news article, copy it neatly onto a separate sheet of paper. Write a new headline for your story. You can also use a computer to make your final copy.

© Harcourt

Challenge
Lead the Way

Name _____

We're Alike but Different—
Who Are We?

Some topics naturally lend themselves to comparison and contrast. It's easy to see why you might compare and contrast a lemon and a lime or football with soccer. What about when you compare wrestling with ballet or a piano with an accordion? You might need to look more closely to see the similarities or differences. Examine some unusual pairs. Then write riddles to help others see how you compare and contrast them.

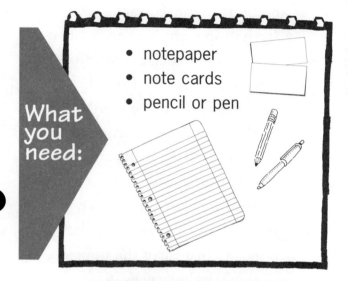

What you need:

- notepaper
- note cards
- pencil or pen

One of us tells tales with words on a page, the other with pictures on a screen. Who are we?

a book and a movie

What to do:

1. Choose pairs of objects, ideas, or activities to compare and contrast. Be creative. On a separate sheet of paper, make a list of at least ten pairs.

2. Write riddles that compare and contrast each pair. Do not name the items in your clues.

3. Copy each riddle onto a note card. Write the answer on the back of the card.

4. Share your riddles with your classmates.

© Harcourt

87

Word Mini-Book

How do you find the meaning of a word? One way is to look up the word in a dictionary. A more thorough way is to make a word mini-book. A word map lets you create a more complete definition of a word than most dictionaries have.

What you need:

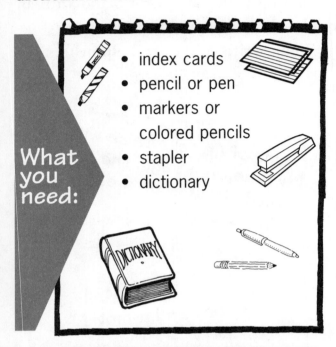

- index cards
- pencil or pen
- markers or colored pencils
- stapler
- dictionary

What to do:

1. Write each Vocabulary Word on a separate index card. On the back of each card, make a large plus sign that divides the card into four quarters.

2. • In the top left corner, define the Vocabulary Word. Use a dictionary if necessary.
- In the top right corner, list two words you associate with the Vocabulary Word. Provide definitions for these words.
- In the bottom left corner, write a sentence using the Vocabulary Word.
- In the bottom right corner, list two words that mean the opposite or nearly the opposite of the Vocabulary Word.

3. Use a blank index card to create a cover for your mini-book. Include a title and an illustration. Staple the cards together to create a vocabulary mini-book.

Challenge
Lead the Way

Fire Flowchart

Imagine that you belong to the city firefighting team in "Fire!" What is your average day like? Use the information in the selection to write and illustrate a flowchart.

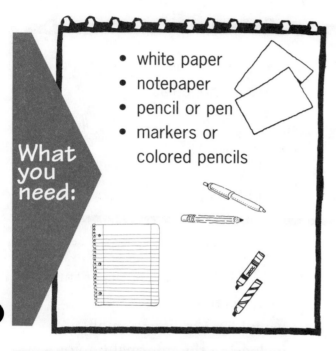

What you need:

- white paper
- notepaper
- pencil or pen
- markers or colored pencils

What to do:

1. Look over the first six pages of "Fire!" Make a list of the things that firefighters do during a 24-hour shift.

2. On your white paper, draw a box for each activity the firefighters complete during their shift. Draw arrows between the boxes. Fill in each box with an activity. Arrange the activities in the order you think they would happen during a shift. Be sure to mention the different roles firefighters play when they fight a fire. Include simple things, such as arriving at the firehouse, sleeping, and eating.

3. Illustrate each box with a drawing. Display your flowchart on a classroom bulletin board.

Challenge
Lead the Way

Name _____

Create a Pamphlet

Reference sources such as encyclopedias, atlases, and almanacs provide information about many topics. Use an encyclopedia to research a topic that interests you. Then create a pamphlet with the information you find.

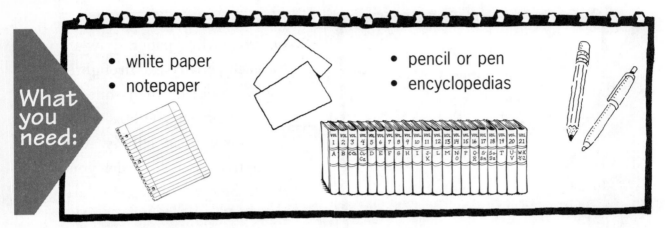

What you need:

- white paper
- notepaper

- pencil or pen
- encyclopedias

What to do:

1. Choose a topic you would like to research. Write the topic on your notepaper.

2. Find your topic in an encyclopedia. List three facts about the topic on your notepaper. Find three related topics, and list them on your notepaper.

3. Fold a sheet of white paper into three sections to make a pamphlet. On your pamphlet, include all the information you collected. Add headings and illustrations to show examples or to explain aspects of the topic.

4. Present your pamphlet to the class. Remember to explain your illustrations.

Challenge
Lead the Way

Build a Word

All the words in the English language are made by combining the same twenty-six letters in different ways. You can build new words by putting the letters in the Vocabulary Words in different order.

| apologized | obliged | certificate | examiner |
| petitioners | resounded | enrich | |

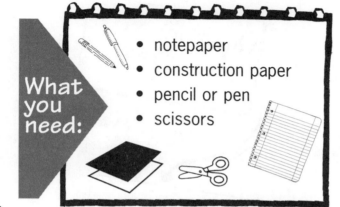

What you need:

- notepaper
- construction paper
- pencil or pen
- scissors

What to do:

1. Cut squares out of construction paper. The squares should be about two inches across. Write each of the letters in the Vocabulary Word on a separate square.

2. Move the squares around to build new words. You don't have to use all the letters in each new word, but you can work only with the letters you have. Form as many new words as you can. An example for *apologized* is *loop*. Write your new words on a sheet of paper.

3. Repeat the steps for each Vocabulary Word. You can reuse some of your letter squares each time, but you also will have to write new ones.

Challenge
Lead the Way

Author Talk

Suppose author Maggie Rugg Herold is visiting your local bookstore. Your school newspaper has asked you to interview Ms. Herold. In particular, they would like you to find out why Ms. Herold wrote "A Very Important Day."

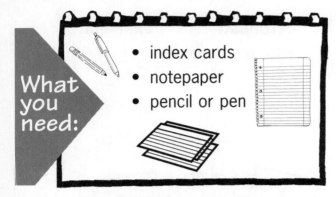

What you need:
- index cards
- notepaper
- pencil or pen

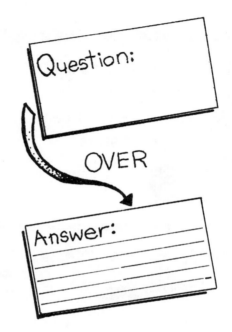

Question:

OVER

Answer:

What to do:

1. Review "A Very Important Day." Think about the author's purpose and the events and details that support that purpose. What additional information would you like to find out about why she wrote this book?

2. Make a list of questions you would ask in your interview. Remember to ask questions about Ms. Herold's background or events in her life that might have led her to write the book. Write each question on an index card. Then imagine you are the author. Write the answers to the questions on the back of your cards.

3. Evaluate your interview. Did you clearly identify the author's purpose? Did you find appropriate details and background information to support your conclusions? Write an article for the newspaper summarizing your interview.

© Harcourt

Challenge
Lead the Way

You're the Teacher

You can pretend you are a teacher giving a test. Write your own test with questions about "A Very Important Day."

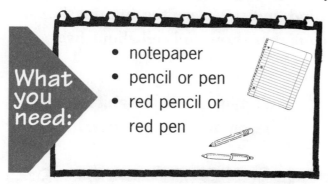

What you need:

- notepaper
- pencil or pen
- red pencil or red pen

What to do:

1. Divide the selection into parts. Reread each part.

2. Write three questions about each section. Your questions should focus on important events and details. Write more than one type of question, such as multiple choice, true/false, fill-in-the-blank, and short answer.

3. Make an answer key for your test. Suggest a strategy that would be helpful in answering each question, such as *look for key words*, *read the question carefully*, or *look for sequence*. Write the strategy next to the question.

Challenge
Lead the Way

Shape Poems

People say that a picture is worth a thousand words. Some words, such as those for people, places, or things, are easy to show with pictures. Other words are harder to see in your mind, but these are the fun ones! Use your imagination to make shape poems that show and tell about five Vocabulary Words.

brush	spiny	teeming	habitat
topple	decomposes	perch	nectar

What you need:

- white paper
- notepaper
- poster board
- scissors
- pencil or pen
- markers or colored pencils
- tape or glue

What to do:

1. Choose five Vocabulary Words. Brainstorm the shapes and pictures that the Vocabulary Words bring to mind.

2. Choose one shape for each Vocabulary Word. Sketch the shapes on a sheet of white paper. Cut out the shapes.

3. Write a short poem about each Vocabulary Word. The poems don't have to rhyme. Copy your poems on the shapes. Try to arrange the lines of each poem so they match their shapes.

4. Decorate your shape poems with the pictures you brainstormed earlier. Tape or glue the shape poems to a piece of poster board. Below each shape poem, write the Vocabulary Word it describes, along with a definition of the word.

© Harcourt

Challenge
Lead the Way

Cactus Creatures

Nonfiction writing is found in books, encyclopedias, newspapers, and magazines. Its main purpose is often to give information about a topic, and it is often organized by main idea and details. Make a nonfiction poster about the animals that depend on the saguaro cactus for survival.

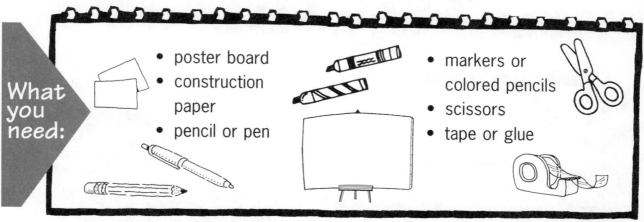

What you need:

- poster board
- construction paper
- pencil or pen
- markers or colored pencils
- scissors
- tape or glue

What to do:

1. Choose two animals from the selection that live in or use the saguaro cactus. On a piece of poster board, draw a picture of the cactus and the two animals. Show how each animal uses the cactus.

2. Review the selection to find a main idea about each animal. Write each main idea on a strip of construction paper. Write the details that support each main idea on strips of construction paper.

3. Tape or glue the main ideas and details beneath the drawings they describe. Display your poster in your classroom.

Which animals depend on me?

Challenge
Lead the Way

Name _____

RE +

The usual way to write words is with letters. A fun way is to make a rebus. A rebus uses letters and pictures that show a word's sound. Use your imagination, and make rebuses for the Vocabulary Words.

sulkily	indifferent	undoubtedly	heartily
protruded	loathe	certainly	

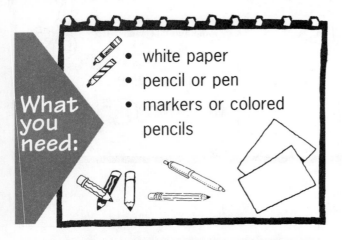

What you need:

- white paper
- pencil or pen
- markers or colored pencils

What to do:

1. Choose five Vocabulary Words to make into rebuses. Here is an example of a rebus for *heartily:*

2. Think of a combination of letters and pictures to show the sounds of three other Vocabulary Words. Use addition signs to put the letters and pictures together for each word. If a picture has an extra sound that is not in the Vocabulary Word, use a subtraction sign to show that the sound is taken out.

3. Draw each rebus on a sheet of white paper.

© Harcourt

Challenge
Lead the Way

A Change of Purpose

If authors had no purpose for their writing, readers would not know whether an author meant to inform them, to entertain them, or to persuade them. A different purpose can give a whole new meaning to a piece of writing. Experiment with different purposes to see how an article's meaning can change.

What you need:

- old children's newspapers or magazines
- notepaper
- pencil or pen

What to do:

1. Look through the magazines or newspapers for a short article that interests you. Read the article, and determine whether the author's purpose was to inform, to entertain, or to persuade.

2. Rewrite the article in your own words, but choose a different purpose.

3. Write a paragraph about how the purpose you chose changed the meaning of the original article.

Challenge
Lead the Way

Name _____

What I Said Is Not What I Meant!

Imagine the confusion that words with multiple meanings would cause if we had no way of knowing which meaning was meant. In this activity, you can create a little confusion on purpose by providing the wrong definitions for some multiple-meaning words.

What you need:

- paper
- pencil or pen

What to do:

1. Brainstorm a list of five to ten words that have more than one meaning. Write two possible definitions for each word. Try to do this without looking in a dictionary.

2. Write a letter to a friend. Write about any topic, but use each of your multiple-meaning words in the body of the letter.

3. Copy the letter to your friend on another sheet of paper. This time, add the element of confusion. Each time you come to one of your multiple-meaning words, replace it with its other definition. Place parentheses around each definition.

4. Read your letter out loud and listen to your confusing sentences.

Challenge
Lead the Way

Name _____

What's in a Name?

Each Vocabulary Word in this lesson is a noun, a word that names a person, a place, a thing, or an idea. You know the basic meanings of the Vocabulary Words. Now try writing a definition poem for each.

culture	accordion	confetti	mesquite	barbecue	chile

What you need:
- pencil or pen
- index cards

What to do:

1. At the top of each index card, write one of the following phrases:
   Culture is . . .
   Mesquite is . . .
   An **accordion** is . . .
   A **barbecue** is . . .
   Confetti is . . .
   A **chile** is . . . .

2. Brainstorm a list of words, phrases, ideas, and images that tell about the person, place, thing, or idea the Vocabulary Word names.

3. Use your list to write a four-line poem for each word, describing what the person, place, thing, or idea is or what it means to you.

Culture is...

Challenge
Lead the Way

Name _____

Favorite Recipe

Everyone has favorite foods or special meals for holidays. Do you know how to make any of the foods you enjoy? Could you explain the steps in sequence? Remember, sequence is the order in which things happen.

What you need:

- pencil or pen
- index card
- cookbooks

- computer with Internet access

What to do:

1. Think of a food you enjoy for a special meal or a particular holiday. Use a cookbook or an Internet search engine to find a recipe for the food.

2. Read the recipe. Note the sequence of steps. Pay attention to numbers marking the steps. Also look for signal words or phrases, such as *first*, *then*, *next*, and *last*.

3. List the steps in order on the index card. Add a signal word or phrase to begin each sentence.

© Harcourt

Challenge
Lead the Way

Name _____

Tales of a Gold Miner

One way that we find out about the lives of gold miners is through the journals and letters they wrote at the time. Imagine that your family has gone to California to pan for gold. Write a journal about your adventures.

beckons   abandoned   multicultural

profitable   fares   rugged

 **What you need:**

- white paper
- construction paper
- pencil or pen

- markers or colored pencils
- stapler

What to do:

1. Fold several sheets of white paper in half to form a journal.

2. On each page of the journal, write an entry. Give each entry a date, and use a Vocabulary Word in each entry. Use the word in a way that shows its meaning. Draw illustrations of your adventures for your journal.

3. Fold a piece of construction paper in half to make a cover for your journal. Decorate the cover with an illustration. Slip the folded white paper inside the cover you made, and staple the pages together.

© Harcourt

Challenge
Lead the Way

Mining Facts and Opinions

Facts are statements that can be proved. Opinions are ideas, thoughts, and personal beliefs. Opinions are different for every person. Make your own gold-mining equipment to separate facts from opinions.

What you need:

- brown, yellow, and orange construction paper
- scissors

- pencil or pen
- tape or glue

What to do:

1. Study the picture of the gold pan in "The Gold Rush." Then draw the shape of a gold pan on a sheet of brown construction paper. Place a second sheet of brown construction paper under the first. Cut out two gold pans.

2. Cut a sheet of yellow construction paper into eight sections to make gold nuggets. Cut a sheet of orange construction paper into eight sections to make pieces of fool's gold.

3. Look in "The Gold Rush" for examples of facts and opinions. Write each fact on a gold nugget, and write each opinion on a piece of fool's gold.

4. Tape or glue the gold nuggets to one gold pan and the fool's gold to the other pan. Display your gold pans in your classroom.

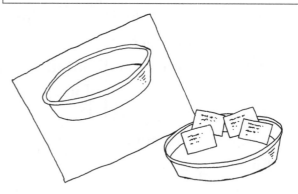

Challenge
Lead the Way

Name _____

Outlines Are Golden

There are many uses for outlines. As you do research, you can take notes in outline form. You can make an outline to help you write a story or a research paper. Outlining a chapter in a textbook will help you focus on the most important information so that you can study for a test. Practice your outlining skills with a magazine or newspaper article.

What you need:
- magazine or newspaper
- pencil or pen
- notepaper

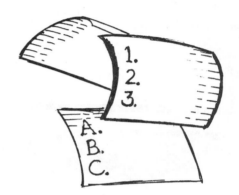

What to do:

1. Choose a magazine or newspaper article to outline. Read it carefully.

2. Find the most important ideas in the article. If the article is divided into sections, each section probably has a main idea. If the sections have headings, they probably give clues to the main ideas.

3. Find the details that support each main idea. Decide whether any of these details can be divided into more than one idea.

4. On a sheet of notepaper, write an outline of the article. Make the main ideas the main items in your outline. Make the details and supporting ideas the other items in your outline. Then write a title for your outline. This can be the title of the original article or a new title.

Challenge
Lead the Way

Vocabulary Poems

One way to practice your Vocabulary Words from "I Have Heard of a Land" is to write a poem that uses all of them.

| pioneer | fertile | arbor | harmony | possibilities |

What you need:

- paper
- pencil or pen
- markers or colored pencils
- dictionary

What to do:

1. On a sheet of paper, write each Vocabulary Word and its definition. Use a dictionary if necessary.

2. Brainstorm a list of images that you associate with each Vocabulary Word.

3. Use each Vocabulary Word and related words from your list to write a five-line poem.

4. Use markers or colored pencils to illustrate your poem.

Challenge
Lead the Way

© Harcourt

Name _____

Word Pyramid

One way to explore the meaning of a word is to think about how it is related to other words you know. Follow the instructions below to explore word relationships in a word pyramid.

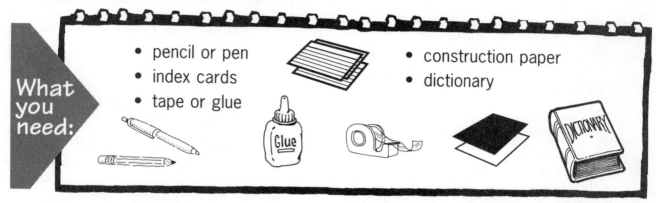

What you need:
- pencil or pen
- index cards
- tape or glue
- construction paper
- dictionary

What to do:

1. Look back at "I Have Heard of a Land." Find a word that is made up of other words that you know (for example, *outdoor*). Write the word on an index card. Then write its definition on the back of the card. Use a dictionary if necessary.

2. Brainstorm a list of words related to the word you have chosen (for example: *doorway, outside,* and *without*). Write each of these words on separate index cards. On the back of each card, write the definition. Use a dictionary if necessary.

3. Place the cards of the related words on your desk, definition side up. Below each definition, write how the word is related to the word you picked from "I Have Heard of a Land." (For example, *outside* and *outdoor* both refer to something that is not inside. A *doorway* separates *outdoor* from *indoor.*)

4. Use the cards to build a word pyramid. Place the word from the story (*outdoor*) at the very top center of your desk. Arrange the related words below it. Line up the word parts that the words share. Tape or glue your word pyramid to a sheet of construction paper.

Challenge
Lead the Way

Paraphrase Practice

Copy a magazine article or an encyclopedia entry, and put it in your
own words.

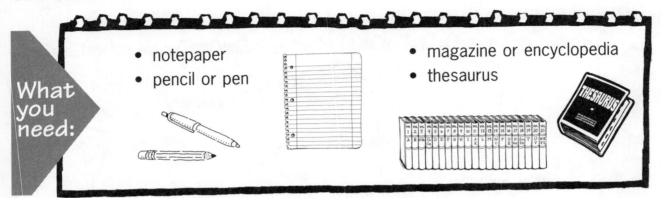

What you need:

- notepaper
- pencil or pen

- magazine or encyclopedia
- thesaurus

What to do:

1. Find a magazine article or
   encyclopedia entry that interests
   you. Choose two paragraphs from
   the article or entry to copy. Write
   each sentence on a separate line
   of your notepaper.

2. In the blank space after each
   sentence, paraphrase what is
   written. Experiment with using
   synonyms and changing sentence
   structure. Make sure your
   paraphrase is nearly the same
   length as the original. Use a
   thesaurus if necessary.

3. When you have finished, recopy
   your paraphrase on a clean sheet
   of paper. Read the original
   paragraphs to friends, and then
   read the paraphrase.

Challenge
Lead the Way

Vocabulary Bull's-Eye

A bull's-eye is the center of a round target. Several circles surround the bull's-eye, each a little farther away from the center. You can create a vocabulary bull's-eye with a Vocabulary Word in the center and information about the Vocabulary Word in the surrounding circles.

bellowing	softhearted	ration
tragedy	fateful	gadgets

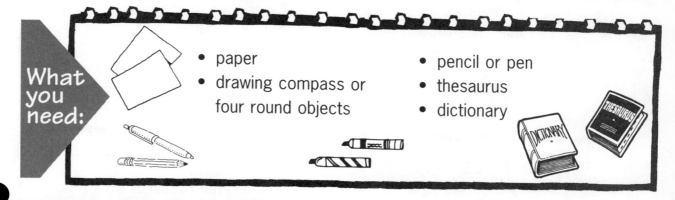

What you need:

- paper
- drawing compass or four round objects
- pencil or pen
- thesaurus
- dictionary

What to do:

1. Use a drawing compass to draw a small circle, about 1 inch across, in the middle of a sheet of paper. If you don't have a drawing compass, you can trace a round object. Draw a second circle, about 3 inches across, around the first one. Draw a third circle, about 5 inches across, around the second one. Draw a fourth circle, about 7 inches across, around the third one.

2. In the center of the target, write a Vocabulary Word. Write synonyms of the word in the second circle. Use a thesaurus to help you. In the third circle, write what the word means. Use a dictionary to find the definition. In the fourth circle, write a sentence using the word.

3. Make a bull's-eye target for each Vocabulary Word.

© Harcourt

Challenge
Lead the Way

Lakes of Fact and Opinion

People say that many lakes in Wisconsin and Minnesota were made from Babe the Blue Ox's footprints. That is an opinion on how these lakes came to be. You can find examples of both facts and opinions in "Paul Bunyan and Babe the Blue Ox."

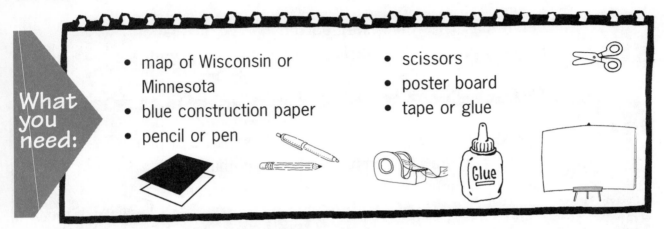

What you need:

- map of Wisconsin or Minnesota
- blue construction paper
- pencil or pen
- scissors
- poster board
- tape or glue

What to do:

1. Locate several lakes on a map of Wisconsin or Minnesota. Study their shapes. Use the shapes on the map as a guide. Draw at least five lakes on blue construction paper, and cut them out.

2. Find examples of fact and opinion in "Paul Bunyan and Babe the Blue Ox." Write a fact or an opinion on each lake. Name each lake according to the fact or opinion you write.

3. Tape or glue the lakes on a piece of poster board. Arrange them the same way they are on the map. Below each lake, write how you know whether the quote is a fact or an opinion.

© Harcourt

Challenge
Lead the Way

Riddle Me This

Everyone tells riddles. They're funny, and they allow people to laugh together. Riddles can be useful, too. You can make up your own riddles to help you remember the meanings of the Vocabulary Words.

boggiest	dissolve	chemicals	carnivorous
accidentally	fertilizer	victim	

What you need:

- notepaper
- white paper
- construction paper

- pencil or pen
- markers or colored pencils
- stapler

What to do:

1. Write a riddle for each of the Vocabulary Words. You can give a clue about the word, you can make a joke about the sound of the word, or you can say something funny about the word.

2. Copy your riddles on separate sheets of white paper. On each sheet of paper, draw a picture that illustrates the riddle. The picture can show the meaning of the word, or it can be part of the joke.

3. Now put your riddles together to make a book. Use construction paper to make a cover for your riddle book. Decorate the cover, and draw a picture. Give your riddle book a title, and write it on the cover. Staple together the sheets of white paper and the cover.

Name _____

The Root of the Matter

Where did root words come from? Many root words came to the English language from ancient languages, such as Latin or Greek. You can research the origins of words to learn more about them.

What you need:

- dictionary or Internet access
- pencil or pen
- notepaper

What to do:

1. Think of words you know that sound similar. For example, the words *vision* and *visible* both have the root *vis* in them. Think of five word pairs or word groups made up of similar-sounding words.

2. Write down the definitions of these words. You can use a dictionary to help you. Then find out whether these words are related. Look in a dictionary or on the Internet to find out the origins of the words.

3. Compare the words in each pair or group. Ask yourself these questions:
- Do these words have related meanings?
- Do these words have the same root word?
- Did these words come to the English language from the same language?

4. If the answer to all these questions is *yes*, then the words are related. If not, they just sound similar. Write a paragraph about what you learned.

Challenge
Lead the Way

The Visual Dictionary

Is it possible to learn a new word without the definition? One of the best ways to learn a new word is to have it illustrated for you. You can illustrate the Vocabulary Words with pictures so that others can learn their meanings.

transformed	investigate	enthusiastically
decor	apparently	corridor

What you need:

- construction paper
- white paper
- old magazines

- scissors
- markers or colored pencils
- tape or glue

What to do:

1. For each Vocabulary Word, think of an illustration that will show its meaning.

2. Look in old magazines to cut out pictures that will help you create your illustration. You may need to combine parts of different pictures to create the picture you want.

3. On white paper, draw additional pictures to help illustrate each word, or draw a background for your illustration.

4. Tape or glue the magazine pictures and your drawings on separate sheets of construction paper. At the top of each illustration, write the word you have illustrated and a few sentences that explain how your illustration shows the meaning of the word. Staple the sheets of construction paper together to make a booklet.

Challenge
Lead the Way

Name _____

Your Advertising Agency

Imagine that you are the owner of an advertising agency. The director of a nearby animal shelter has asked you to create an advertisement to put in newspapers and magazines. Create three sample advertisements. One should *persuade* people to visit the animal shelter, one should *entertain* people with a story or poem about the animals, and one should *inform* people about the shelter and its facilities. Each advertisement needs both words and art.

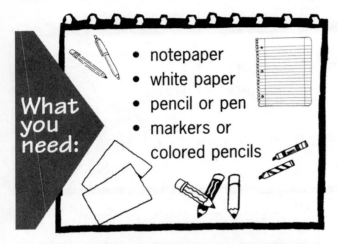

What you need:

- notepaper
- white paper
- pencil or pen
- markers or colored pencils

What to do:

1. Write the text for the three advertisements. Make up the actual animal shelter information, such as the hours of operation, the location, and the animals that live there.

2. Create an advertisement for each purpose. Consider the following things as you design each advertisement:
   - How should I combine the text and the art?
   - What colors and letter styles will work well for each purpose?
   - Have I created material that will appeal to a large number of people with different interests?

3. On the back of each advertisement, write a brief explanation of how the advertisement you designed meets its intended purpose of persuading, entertaining, or informing.

ANIMAL SHELTER

© Harcourt

Challenge
Lead the Way

Page 15
1. valuable; sportsmanship
2. tremendous; monster, dune
3. appreciation; courageous
4. immigrants; I, mints, gram
5. salary; modest; ode

Challenge
Lead the Way